Luke Evans

Luke George Evans: A Journey Through Stage and Screen

Early Life and Education

Born on Easter Sunday, April 15, 1979, in Pontypool, Wales, Luke George Evans grew up in the small town of Aberbargoed. As the only child of Yvonne and David Evans, Luke's early years were shaped by his upbringing as a Jehovah's Witness. However, at the age of 16, he chose to leave both the religion and his schooling behind. Seeking a new path, he moved to Cardiff at 17 and began studying under the guidance of singing coach Louise Ryan. His dedication paid off when he won a scholarship to the prestigious London Studio Centre in 1997, from which he graduated in 2000.

The Stage: Where It All Began

Evans' career began on the vibrant stages of London's West End. From 2000 to 2008, he shone in numerous productions, including "La Cava," "Taboo," "Rent," "Miss Saigon," and "Avenue Q." His performances in fringe shows in London and at the Edinburgh Festival also garnered acclaim. In 2008, Evans landed a significant role in Peter Gill's play "Small Change" at the Donmar Warehouse. His portrayal of Vincent captured the attention of film casting directors and U.S. talent agencies, earning him a nomination for the Evening Standard Award for Outstanding Newcomer. That same year, he took on the role of Yves Montand in "Piaf" at the Donmar Warehouse.

Breaking into Film

At age 30, Evans had his first film audition and soon after, his first film role. In 2009, he was cast as the Greek god Apollo in the 2010 remake of "Clash of the Titans." This was just the beginning. In 2010 alone, Evans appeared in "Sex & Drugs & Rock & Roll," "Robin Hood," and "Tamara Drewe," showcasing his versatility as an actor.

Rising Star in Hollywood

Evans' breakout year came in 2011 with roles in "Blitz," "The Three Musketeers," and "Immortals," where he played Zeus. He continued to build his filmography with performances in "The Raven" (2012) and "No One Lives" (2012). However, it was his role as Bard the Bowman in Peter Jackson's "The Hobbit" trilogy (2012-2014) and as Owen Shaw in "Fast & Furious 6" (2013) that cemented his status as a Hollywood star.

In 2014, Evans took on the iconic role of Dracula in "Dracula Untold," further showcasing his ability to lead major motion pictures. His portrayal of Gaston in Disney's live-action "Beauty and the Beast" (2017) alongside Emma Watson and Dan Stevens brought him into the hearts of a new generation of fans. The same year, he starred as William Moulton Marston in the biographical drama "Professor Marston and the Wonder Women."

Continued Success and Diversification

Evans continued to diversify his roles, starring in thrillers like "The Girl on the Train" (2016) and war movies like "Midway" (2019). He also ventured into television, playing key roles in series such as "The Alienist" (2018-2020), "The Pembrokeshire Murders" (2020), and "Nine Perfect Strangers" (2021).

Music and Personal Life

Aside from acting, Luke Evans is also a talented singer. He released his debut album, "At Last," on November 22, 2019, followed by "A Song for You" in 2022. His musical endeavors showcase yet another facet of his artistic talent.

Evans is openly gay but prefers to keep his personal life private. He believes that his talent and success should not be influenced by his private life. He has had high-profile relationships, including with actor and model Jon Kortajarena and, since 2021, with Fran Tomas.

Legacy and Future

Luke Evans has proven himself a versatile and talented performer, seamlessly transitioning from stage to screen and from acting to singing. With a career spanning over two decades, he continues to captivate audiences worldwide with his dynamic performances and charismatic presence. As he continues to take on diverse roles in film and television, Luke Evans remains a prominent figure in the entertainment industry, inspiring many with his journey from a small Welsh town to international stardom.

A Journey Beyond Boundaries

Evans' career trajectory knows no bounds. With each new project, he pushes the boundaries of his craft, captivating audiences with his versatility and depth. His foray into voice acting, including roles in animated films like "StarDog and TurboCat" (2019) and "Scrooge: A Christmas Carol" (2022), further demonstrates his ability to inhabit characters of all kinds, even those unseen.

In 2022, Evans took on the role of The Coachman in Robert Zemeckis' live-action adaptation of Disney's "Pinocchio," showcasing his ability to bring beloved characters to life with his signature flair. This was followed by his portrayal of Ebenezer Scrooge in "Scrooge: A Christmas Carol," adding a fresh perspective to a timeless tale.

A Vision for Tomorrow

As Evans' career evolves, he continues to challenge himself with new projects and collaborations. His upcoming roles in films like "5lbs of Pressure" (2024) and "World Breaker" (TBA) promise to push the boundaries of storytelling even further, solidifying his status as a versatile and enduring talent in the industry.

Beyond his artistic endeavors, Evans remains committed to using his platform for positive change. Whether advocating for LGBTQ+ rights or supporting charitable causes, he leverages his influence to make a difference in the world.

Conclusion

From his humble beginnings in Wales to his ascent to international stardom, Luke George Evans' journey is one of resilience, talent, and determination. With each performance, he invites audiences into worlds both familiar and fantastical, leaving an indelible mark on the hearts and minds of viewers around the globe.

As he continues to captivate audiences with his magnetic presence and multifaceted talents, Luke Evans stands as a testament to the power of passion, perseverance, and the relentless pursuit of one's dreams. And as the curtain rises on the next chapter of his remarkable journey, one thing remains certain: the world eagerly awaits to see what heights he will conquer next.

The Advocate and Role Model
While Evans continues to excel in his professional life, he has also embraced his role as an advocate and role model within the LGBTQ+ community. Despite the scrutiny that often comes with fame, Evans has remained steadfast in his belief that his private life should remain private, stating, "Talent, success, what you do in your personal life – I don't see how one should have an effect on the other." This philosophy has allowed him to maintain a sense of normalcy and groundedness despite his rising fame.

His openness about his sexuality, combined with his refusal to let it define his career, has made him a powerful figure in Hollywood. In an industry that is still grappling with issues of representation and inclusivity, Evans stands out as a beacon of authenticity and integrity. His relationship with Spanish model Fran Tomas, which began in 2021, has been another testament to his approach to love and life – one that is lived authentically but privately.

Discography and Musical Talent
Evans' musical talents, showcased in his studio albums "At Last" (2019) and "A Song for You" (2022), have added another layer to his multifaceted career. His music, characterized by a rich, soulful voice and a deep emotional resonance, has been well received by fans and critics alike. Songs like "Love Is a Battlefield" and "Come What May" (featuring Charlotte Church) highlight his ability to convey powerful emotions through music.

Evans' musical journey has also included live performances, such as "At Last! The Live Tour" in 2021, where he connected with audiences on a personal level, sharing his love for music and performing.

Future Projects and Aspirations
Looking ahead, Luke Evans continues to take on projects that challenge and inspire him. His upcoming miniseries "The Way," where he plays Hogwood, and his role in "Our Son" (2023) alongside Billy Porter, are highly anticipated. Each new role allows Evans to explore different facets of his craft, from intense drama to thrilling action.

In addition to his acting and singing careers, Evans is also exploring opportunities behind the camera. He has expressed interest in producing and directing, aiming to bring compelling and diverse stories to life. This evolution in his career marks a natural progression for an artist who has always sought to expand his horizons and take creative risks.

Personal Philosophy and Legacy

Evans' journey is characterized by a profound personal philosophy that emphasizes authenticity, resilience, and a relentless pursuit of excellence. His story is a testament to the idea that true success comes not just from talent, but from integrity and the courage to stay true to oneself.

As he continues to build on his impressive body of work, Luke Evans remains a figure of inspiration for aspiring actors, musicians, and anyone striving to follow their dreams. His legacy is one of versatility, passion, and an unwavering commitment to his craft.

The Story Continues

Luke George Evans' story is far from over. With every new role, song, and project, he continues to captivate and inspire. Whether on stage, on screen, or in the recording studio, Evans brings a unique blend of talent, charisma, and authenticity that resonates with audiences around the world.

As he forges ahead, exploring new creative territories and breaking new ground, Luke Evans remains a shining example of what it means to be an artist in the truest sense. His journey is a remarkable tale of dedication, passion, and the enduring power of the human spirit – a story that will undoubtedly continue to unfold in exciting and unexpected ways.

A Champion of Diverse Narratives

Luke Evans is not just an actor and singer; he is a storyteller who seeks out roles and projects that highlight diverse narratives. His performances often delve into complex characters and rich storylines, reflecting his deep commitment to bringing varied human experiences to the forefront.

Exploring New Genres

Evans' willingness to explore a wide range of genres has set him apart in the industry. From historical epics like "Clash of the Titans" and "Immortals" to the supernatural in "Dracula Untold" and psychological thrillers like "The Girl on the Train," Evans has demonstrated a remarkable ability to adapt and excel. His upcoming projects, such as the black ops military series "Echo 3" and the psychological drama "Our Son," promise to continue this trend of versatile and compelling performances.

A Return to Theater?

While Evans has made a significant impact in film and television, he has expressed a desire to return to his theatrical roots. The stage, where he first honed his craft, holds a special place in his heart. There is anticipation among fans and industry insiders alike about the potential for Evans to take on new stage roles, perhaps even in original productions or revivals of classic plays. His powerful stage presence and dynamic performances in theater have left a lasting legacy, and a return would undoubtedly be welcomed.

Philanthropy and Advocacy

Outside of his professional endeavors, Luke Evans is known for his philanthropic efforts. He actively supports various charities and causes, particularly those related to LGBTQ+ rights, mental health, and the arts. His involvement in these causes reflects his belief in giving back to the community and using his platform for positive change.

Evans' work with organizations like The Trevor Project and the British Red Cross highlights his commitment to making a difference. He often participates in charity events, fundraisers, and awareness campaigns, using his influence to advocate for those in need.

Personal Interests and Hobbies

Beyond the glitz and glamour of Hollywood, Luke Evans leads a life enriched by a variety of personal interests and hobbies. He is an avid traveler, often sharing glimpses of his adventures on social media. His love for exploring new cultures and destinations adds another dimension to his vibrant personality.

Evans is also a fitness enthusiast, maintaining a rigorous workout routine that includes weight training, cardio, and outdoor activities. His dedication to health and fitness not only helps him stay in peak physical condition for his demanding roles but also serves as an inspiration to his fans.

A Vision for the Future

As Luke Evans continues to evolve as an artist, he remains focused on the future. His aspirations include expanding his work behind the camera, producing and possibly directing films and series that reflect his diverse interests and commitment to storytelling. This move would allow him to shape narratives from a different perspective and provide opportunities for emerging talents in the industry.

An Enduring Legacy

Luke George Evans' journey from a small Welsh town to international stardom is a testament to his extraordinary talent, hard work, and perseverance. His ability to navigate the complexities of the entertainment industry while staying true to himself has made him a beloved figure worldwide.

As he continues to break new ground and take on challenging roles, Evans' legacy as a versatile and dedicated artist grows stronger. His story is an inspiring example of what can be achieved with passion, integrity, and an unwavering commitment to one's craft.

The Next Chapter

With each new project, Luke Evans adds to his rich tapestry of work, leaving audiences eagerly anticipating what he will do next. Whether it's a new film, a return to the stage, a musical release, or his ventures into production and direction, one thing is certain: Luke Evans will continue to captivate, inspire, and entertain for years to come.

His journey is a dynamic and ongoing narrative, filled with promise and potential. As we look forward to the next chapter in the remarkable story of Luke George Evans, we celebrate not just an exceptional artist, but a genuine and inspiring human being.

Embracing New Horizons

As Luke Evans continues to navigate his illustrious career, he remains open to exploring new horizons. His curiosity and willingness to take on diverse roles have made him a unique figure in the entertainment industry. This openness is not only a testament to his versatility as an actor but also reflects his passion for storytelling in all its forms.

Collaboration and Creativity

Evans values collaboration and often speaks about the importance of working with talented directors, writers, and fellow actors. His career is filled with notable collaborations that have resulted in critically acclaimed performances. Working with visionary directors like Peter Jackson, Bill Condon, and Roland Emmerich, Evans has learned from some of the best in the industry.

His ability to adapt to different styles and genres is partly due to his collaborative spirit. He brings a sense of camaraderie and mutual respect to every project, making him a sought-after collaborator. Whether he is working on a big-budget blockbuster or an independent film, Evans' dedication to the craft and respect for his colleagues shine through.

Music: A Lifelong Passion

Evans' foray into music with his albums "At Last" and "A Song for You" is a continuation of a lifelong passion. His rich baritone voice and emotive performances have earned him accolades in the music industry. Each album is a personal journey, with songs that reflect his experiences and emotions.

In interviews, Evans often talks about how music has been a constant source of joy and solace in his life. Performing live, whether in an intimate setting or a large concert hall, allows him to connect with his audience on a deeply personal level. His music career is not just a side project but a vital part of his artistic expression.

Upcoming Ventures

Looking ahead, Evans has several exciting projects on the horizon. His role in "The Way," a miniseries exploring complex narratives, promises to be another standout performance. The series is expected to delve into themes of morality, identity, and human connection, areas where Evans excels in bringing depth and nuance.

In addition, his involvement in "5lbs of Pressure" and "World Breaker" signals his ongoing commitment to diverse and challenging roles. These projects are expected to showcase different facets of his talent, from intense drama to high-stakes action.

Personal Growth and Reflection

Despite his busy schedule, Evans takes time for personal growth and reflection. He often shares insights about his journey and the lessons he has learned along the way. His grounded nature and introspective outlook make him relatable to his fans and admirers.

Evans emphasizes the importance of staying true to oneself and pursuing passions with dedication and integrity. His story is not just about professional success but also about personal evolution and the pursuit of a fulfilling life.

A Global Icon

Luke Evans' influence extends beyond the entertainment industry. He has become a global icon, known for his contributions to film, music, and advocacy. His reach is international, with fans from all over the world who admire his talent, charisma, and authenticity.

Evans' ability to connect with people from different backgrounds and cultures is a testament to his universal appeal. He represents the idea that true artistry transcends borders and speaks to the shared human experience.

Continuing the Legacy

Continuing the Legacy

As Evans continues to build on his impressive career, he remains focused on leaving a lasting legacy. His work is characterized by a commitment to excellence, a passion for storytelling, and a dedication to authenticity. These qualities ensure that his influence will be felt for generations to come.

Evans' journey is a source of inspiration for aspiring artists and storytellers. His success story encourages others to pursue their dreams with determination and integrity. He has shown that with hard work and perseverance, it is possible to achieve great heights while staying true to oneself.

A Bright Future

The future is bright for Luke George Evans. With each new project, he continues to surprise and delight audiences, solidifying his place as one of the most talented and versatile performers of his generation. His journey is far from over, and fans eagerly anticipate the next chapter in his remarkable story.

Whether through acting, music, or advocacy, Evans will undoubtedly continue to make a significant impact. His legacy is one of passion, creativity, and an unwavering commitment to excellence. As we look forward to what lies ahead, we celebrate the extraordinary achievements of Luke George Evans, a true artist and a remarkable human being.

Future Aspirations: Beyond the Screen and Stage

As Luke George Evans looks to the future, he envisions expanding his horizons beyond the screen and stage. One of his aspirations is to delve deeper into the world of production and direction. Having observed and learned from some of the industry's finest, Evans aims to bring his unique perspective to projects that resonate with his artistic sensibilities. He is particularly interested in stories that push boundaries and challenge conventional narratives, ensuring that diverse voices and experiences are represented.

Mentorship and Empowerment

Evans is also passionate about mentorship. Recognizing the importance of guidance and support in his own journey, he aims to mentor young and emerging talents in the industry. His goal is to empower the next generation of actors, singers, and filmmakers by sharing his knowledge and experiences. He believes in fostering a creative environment where new ideas can flourish and where aspiring artists can find their footing in a competitive industry.

A Continued Commitment to Advocacy

Luke Evans' advocacy work remains a central part of his life. He is committed to using his platform to raise awareness about issues close to his heart. In addition to his work with LGBTQ+ organizations and mental health charities, Evans is exploring ways to support environmental causes and sustainable practices in the film and music industries. His dedication to making a positive impact is unwavering, and he continues to seek out opportunities to contribute meaningfully to society.

Embracing Digital Media

In an era where digital media plays an increasingly significant role, Evans is keen on exploring this landscape. From participating in web series to creating content for streaming platforms, he sees digital media as a powerful tool for storytelling. Evans is intrigued by the potential of virtual reality (VR) and augmented reality (AR) in creating immersive experiences for audiences. By embracing these technologies, he aims to push the boundaries of traditional storytelling and engage with audiences in innovative ways.

Personal Projects and Passions

On a personal level, Evans continues to nurture his various passions. His love for travel remains strong, and he often takes time off to explore new destinations. These travels not only provide him with a sense of adventure but also serve as a source of inspiration for his creative projects. Whether it's hiking in remote landscapes or immersing himself in different cultures, Evans finds joy and inspiration in the world around him.

He is also an avid supporter of the arts and often attends theater performances, art exhibitions, and music concerts. These experiences enrich his understanding of different art forms and fuel his creativity. Evans' appreciation for the arts extends to his personal life, where he enjoys painting and writing as means of self-expression.

A Legacy of Integrity and Passion

As Luke George Evans continues to carve out his path in the entertainment industry, his legacy is defined by integrity, passion, and a relentless pursuit of excellence. He has proven that true success is not just about fame and accolades but about making a meaningful impact through one's work. His journey is a testament to the power of perseverance, authenticity, and dedication to one's craft.

Looking Forward

With a wealth of experience behind him and countless opportunities ahead, Luke Evans stands at the threshold of new adventures. His future projects promise to be as diverse and compelling as his past work, and fans eagerly anticipate the stories he will bring to life. Whether through acting, singing, directing, or advocacy, Evans' contributions to the arts and society continue to inspire and captivate.

Luke George Evans is more than an actor and singer; he is a storyteller, a mentor, an advocate, and a visionary. As he embarks on new endeavors, his legacy grows ever more significant, leaving an indelible mark on the world of entertainment and beyond. The next chapter in his remarkable journey is sure to be filled with innovation, creativity, and a continued commitment to excellence, ensuring that his influence will be felt for many years to come.

An Artistic Renaissance

As Luke George Evans ventures further into the realms of production and direction, he is undergoing an artistic renaissance. His deep understanding of character development, narrative structure, and the emotional core of storytelling equips him to excel behind the camera. Evans is particularly drawn to projects that challenge societal norms and provoke thoughtful discussion. He aims to produce and direct films that not only entertain but also inspire and educate audiences.

Cultivating a Creative Community

Evans is dedicated to cultivating a creative community that nurtures and supports artists from diverse backgrounds. He envisions establishing a production company that champions innovative and original content. This company would provide a platform for emerging talent, offering resources and mentorship to help them realize their creative visions. Evans' commitment to diversity and inclusion is central to this initiative, ensuring that stories from all walks of life are brought to the forefront.

Exploring New Genres

In his continuous quest for growth, Evans is exploring new genres and mediums. He has expressed interest in delving into the world of animation and voice acting, fascinated by the limitless possibilities these mediums offer. Additionally, he is keen on exploring science fiction and fantasy genres, captivated by their ability to transport audiences to entirely new worlds while reflecting on contemporary issues.

Expanding His Musical Horizons

Evans' musical journey is far from over. He plans to collaborate with other artists across various genres, blending his classical training with contemporary sounds. His goal is to produce music that transcends genres and resonates on a deeply emotional level. Evans is also considering a musical theater project, combining his love for acting and singing in a stage production that celebrates the best of both worlds.

Philanthropic Ventures

Beyond his artistic pursuits, Evans is expanding his philanthropic ventures. He is actively involved in several charitable organizations and is exploring ways to create sustainable impact through his efforts. Evans is particularly interested in education initiatives, aiming to provide access to arts education for underprivileged youth. He believes that nurturing creativity from a young age can transform lives and build a more compassionate and innovative society.

A Personal Journey of Growth

On a personal level, Evans continues to prioritize self-growth and reflection. He often engages in activities that promote mental and physical well-being, such as meditation, yoga, and fitness. These practices help him maintain balance in his demanding career and personal life. Evans is also an advocate for mental health awareness, sharing his experiences to help destigmatize mental health issues and encourage others to seek support.

A Beacon of Inspiration

Luke George Evans stands as a beacon of inspiration for many. His journey from a small town in Wales to global stardom is a testament to the power of dreams, hard work, and resilience. He inspires aspiring artists to pursue their passions relentlessly and to remain true to themselves in the face of adversity.

Reflecting on Legacy

Reflecting on his legacy, Evans is mindful of the impact he wants to leave behind. He aspires to be remembered not just for his remarkable performances but for his contributions to the arts and society. Evans' legacy is one of authenticity, compassion, and a relentless pursuit of excellence. His story serves as a reminder that success is not merely measured by accolades but by the positive change one brings to the world.

Embracing the Future

As Luke George Evans looks to the future, he does so with a sense of excitement and purpose. His career is a testament to his versatility and passion, and he remains committed to pushing the boundaries of his craft. Whether through acting, singing, directing, or advocacy, Evans continues to make a profound impact on the world.

The future chapters of Luke George Evans' life promise to be filled with creativity, innovation, and a steadfast dedication to making a difference. His journey is far from over, and the world eagerly awaits the next steps of this extraordinary artist and human being. With each new endeavor, Evans reaffirms his place as a true luminary in the arts, leaving an indelible mark on the hearts and minds of audiences everywhere.

Embracing Innovation: The Role of Technology in Storytelling
As Luke George Evans continues to evolve in his career, he remains open to the role of technology in storytelling. He is particularly interested in the potential of virtual reality (VR) and augmented reality (AR) to create immersive, interactive narratives that push the boundaries of traditional cinema. By experimenting with these cutting-edge technologies, Evans aims to create experiences that deeply engage audiences and offer new ways of exploring complex themes and emotions.

Collaborations and Creative Partnerships
Evans values collaboration and the exchange of ideas. He is always on the lookout for opportunities to work with like-minded creatives who share his passion for innovative storytelling. Whether it's partnering with visionary directors, writers, or fellow actors, Evans believes that collaboration is key to creating groundbreaking work. He is particularly excited about the prospect of international collaborations that bring together diverse cultural perspectives, enriching the storytelling experience.

Commitment to Authentic Representation
A significant aspect of Evans' future projects is his commitment to authentic representation. He is dedicated to ensuring that his work reflects the diversity of the human experience. This involves not only casting decisions but also the stories he chooses to tell and the creative voices he amplifies. Evans is a vocal advocate for greater representation of LGBTQ+ characters and stories in mainstream media, and he actively seeks out projects that align with this mission.

Expanding Artistic Boundaries

Evans' desire to expand his artistic boundaries is evident in his ongoing exploration of various art forms. He is interested in integrating visual arts, dance, and even experimental theater into his projects. By blending different artistic disciplines, he aims to create multi-sensory experiences that challenge traditional notions of storytelling. Evans is particularly drawn to the idea of site-specific performances and installations that transform everyday spaces into dynamic stages.

Nurturing a Global Fanbase

Throughout his career, Luke George Evans has built a loyal global fanbase that spans across continents. He values the support and connection he shares with his fans and is committed to nurturing this relationship. Evans regularly engages with his audience through social media, sharing glimpses of his personal and professional life. He also looks forward to participating in fan conventions and events worldwide, where he can connect with his supporters in person and express his gratitude for their unwavering support.

Personal Fulfillment and Joy

Amidst his professional endeavors, Evans places a high priority on personal fulfillment and joy. He continues to explore hobbies and activities that bring him happiness, whether it's cooking, gardening, or spending time with loved ones. Evans believes that a well-rounded, fulfilling personal life is essential for sustaining creativity and passion in his work.

The Journey Continues

Luke George Evans' journey is a testament to his relentless pursuit of excellence and his unwavering commitment to authenticity. As he continues to explore new horizons, he remains grounded in his core values of integrity, compassion, and innovation. Each new project is an opportunity for Evans to challenge himself, inspire others, and contribute meaningfully to the world of arts and entertainment.

A Legacy of Inspiration

Evans' legacy is one of inspiration and impact. He has shown that it is possible to achieve success while staying true to oneself and using one's platform for good. His story is a beacon of hope for aspiring artists everywhere, proving that with talent, perseverance, and a genuine love for one's craft, dreams can indeed become reality.

The Road Ahead

As Luke George Evans looks ahead, he does so with a sense of anticipation and excitement. The road ahead is filled with endless possibilities, and Evans is ready to embrace each opportunity with passion and dedication. His future projects will undoubtedly continue to captivate audiences, challenge conventions, and leave an indelible mark on the arts.

With a rich past to reflect upon and a promising future to look forward to, Luke George Evans stands as a true luminary in the world of entertainment. His journey is far from over, and the world eagerly awaits the next chapter in the remarkable story of this extraordinary artist and human being. The best, it seems, is yet to come.

Charting New Territories

With an unwavering spirit of exploration, Luke George Evans remains dedicated to charting new territories in his career. As he ventures into producing and directing, Evans is keen to tell stories that might otherwise be overlooked. He is particularly interested in narratives that highlight marginalized voices and address social issues, using his influence to shine a light on important, yet often ignored, subjects.

Environmental Advocacy

Another emerging passion for Evans is environmental advocacy. He recognizes the urgency of addressing climate change and the responsibility of public figures to lead by example. Evans plans to use his platform to raise awareness about environmental issues and support initiatives aimed at conservation and sustainability. He is considering producing documentaries that explore the impacts of climate change and the efforts being made to combat it, hoping to inspire action and change through compelling storytelling.

Mentorship and Education

Believing in the power of mentorship, Evans is committed to giving back to the next generation of artists. He envisions establishing scholarship programs and workshops that provide aspiring actors and filmmakers with the tools and opportunities they need to succeed. Evans' own experiences have taught him the value of guidance and support, and he is eager to pass on the wisdom he has gained throughout his career.

Expanding His Discography

Evans' musical journey continues to flourish. He is exploring the idea of a follow-up album that dives deeper into his personal experiences and emotions. This album will likely feature original songs written by Evans, showcasing his talents not just as a performer but as a songwriter. Collaborations with other artists across genres are also on the horizon, as Evans seeks to create music that resonates with a wide audience.

Film and Television Ventures

Looking ahead, Evans has a slate of film and television projects that promise to further solidify his reputation as a versatile and compelling actor. These include both leading roles in major studio productions and more intimate, character-driven indie films. His choices reflect a desire to balance commercial success with artistic integrity, always seeking roles that challenge him and offer new perspectives.

The Power of Storytelling

At the heart of Evans' career is a profound belief in the power of storytelling. Whether through film, music, or theater, he understands that stories have the ability to connect people, evoke empathy, and inspire change. Evans is dedicated to using his skills and platform to tell stories that matter, ones that have the potential to make a lasting impact on society.

Personal Life and Balance

Balancing a demanding career with a fulfilling personal life remains a priority for Evans. He cherishes the time spent with family and friends and makes a conscious effort to maintain this balance. Evans' relationship with Fran Tomas has brought him joy and stability, and he values the support and love they share. This personal happiness fuels his professional endeavors, giving him the strength and inspiration to continue pursuing his dreams.

Awards and Recognition

While Evans does not chase accolades, his talent and hard work have not gone unnoticed. He has received numerous awards and nominations throughout his career, a testament to his dedication and skill. These accolades, while appreciated, serve as a reminder of the impact he has made and continue to inspire him to strive for excellence in all his projects.

The Legacy Continues

As Luke George Evans' story unfolds, it is clear that he is a force to be reckoned with in the world of entertainment. His journey from a small town in Wales to international stardom is a remarkable testament to his talent, determination, and authenticity. Evans continues to break boundaries, challenge himself, and inspire others, all while remaining true to his values and passions.

A Bright Future

With numerous projects in the pipeline and an unwavering commitment to his craft, the future looks exceptionally bright for Luke George Evans. His ability to adapt, evolve, and innovate ensures that his career will continue to thrive in the years to come. Fans and audiences worldwide eagerly anticipate the next chapters in Evans' extraordinary journey, confident that he will continue to captivate, inspire, and entertain.

In the world of arts and entertainment, Luke George Evans stands out not only for his remarkable talent but also for his integrity, compassion, and relentless pursuit of excellence. His legacy is one of inspiration and impact, and as he continues to explore new horizons, there is no doubt that he will leave an indelible mark on the hearts and minds of all who experience his work.

Made in the USA
Las Vegas, NV
08 November 2024

11374848R00020